Fennimore Harrison

The Arkansas Traveller

Fennimore Harrison

The Arkansas Traveller

ISBN/EAN: 9783337292287

Printed in Europe, USA, Canada, Australia, Japan

Cover: Foto ©Andreas Hilbeck / pixelio.de

More available books at **www.hansebooks.com**

THE ARKANSAS TRAVELLER;

— A —

NEW ECCENTRIC COMEDY,

— IN —

FOUR ACTS,

— BY —

FENNIMORE HARRISON,

NEW ORLEANS:
1881.

The Arkansas Traveller.

Hello! Stranger!
Hello! yourself!

—:o:—

DRAMATIS PERSONÆ.

HIRAM WARSAW, ... *The Arkansas Traveller.*
SANDY, ... *Owner of the Big Fork Tavern.*
SAMUEL EASY .... *The loquacious toper.*
HEZEKIEL KENT .... *The circuit-rider.*
ALECK FURY .... *The Constable.*
LUCY CRITTENDEN, AND AGNES CRITTENDEN .... *Sisters, from the West, travelling together.*
PHILIP SLY, AND BILLY SHARP .... *Two intrepid tramps from Colorado.*

—:o:—

ACT I.

SCENE—*Interior of Sandy's Big Fork Tavern. Evening.*

Sandy (*listening*). That sounds like the stage-coach (*goes to the door*). No, wrong again. Who's that there? Hey, is that you Sam?

Enter Samuel Easy, smoking a pipe.

Sam. Did you call me? Ain't the stage come yet?

Sandy. No, I'm waitin' for it now; it's high time. Take a seat.

Sam. Well I will, for a rest. You know, Sandy, my wife won't let me alone!

Sandy. What's wrong now?

Sam. She thinks I'm goin' to saw wood before supper! I'm not calcerlated for that. I never could saw wood anyhow!

Sandy. Well, Sam, here's somethin' to make you forgit your troubles. It's a demijug with somethin' in it. Try it!

Sam. Well, Sandy, I can't say as I care very particler just now; however, let me have about a thimbleful.

Sandy. Help yourself. Thar's a glass.

Sam (*Pours out a little and takes it; then fills to the brim*). Sandy, this is a tonic! I didn't know it. It's the real old 'simmon beer!

Sandy. That's some o' mine. We'll have some when the stage comes.

Sam. I'm in dead earnest; it's a tonic! If a man'll stick to 'simmon beer, he'll never be sick any more'n a doctor! Ain't that the stage?

Sandy. It's comin' now, and I'm off to meet it. (*Exit.*)

Sam. Hurry up! You'll be too late; there's somebody gettin' out now. It's a woman!—another woman! Is that all? Here they are.

Enter Lucy and Agnes, with Sandy carrying their carpet-bags.

Agnes. So this is the Big Fork Tavern and the stage stops here all night?

Sandy. This is the Big Fork, strangers, and the stage goin' East always stops here over night. It's the restin' place.

Lucy. That's just what I told you, Agnes; the driver said we'd have to stay here all night and continue the journey in the morning. We'll have to do so.

Sam. It's a mighty good tavern! That 'simmon beer's fust-rate!

Sandy. Oh! I'll be sure to wake you up in time to-morrow mornin'!

Lucy. Yes, you'd better! Agnes and myself are from the West and are going to Kentucky on a visit to some relatives and are going to bring them back with us. Now don't forget it!

Agnes. No indeed!

Sandy. Fix your hopes on me, strangers! I'll tend to every pint. You'll have the best room here, and you'll sleep well, it's so quiet!

Lucy. We don't mind noise; out West people are either fighting or working, and we are used to exciting things.

Sam. You don't fight, do you?

Lucy. I don't mind seeing fights! They give one an appetite!

Sandy. I'm goin' to have supper now, strangers. Hey, Sam, won't you fill this pitcher with fresh water from the well, while I fix the table? (*Prepares the table.*)

Sam. Let me have it. Hello! here comes the Parson with his hick'ry stick!

Enter Hezekiel Kent.

Kent. Wait a minnit, Sam; your wife told me to tell you to come down to the "widders" right off, and help her to tote wood. That's all.

Sam. Parson, I do despise to go near a wood-pile at night—too many snakes. (*Exit.*)

Sandy (*to his guests*). That's Hezekiel Kent, the circuit-rider. (*Kent bows*). And now, strangers, if you'll bring your cheers aroun' this table, we'll try to make you forgit the cares and vexations of travellin'. We'll start to work at once. Come on, Parson.

Lucy. I'm as hungry as a tiger! Are you, Agnes?

Agnes. Of course I am! (*They all sit down.*)

Kent. I 'spose you two ladies are going to stay here always, eh? Then you'd better jine my congregation—contributions only once a month!

Lucy. No, sir; we leave in the morning, but we will give a contribution to a good cause, there!

Kent. Well —

Lucy. Never mind, just take it!

Kent. Thanks! It's really gratifyin' (*puts the coin into his pocket*).

Enter Sam Easy with the water.

Sam. What's that you're up to, Parson? I saw you! No use

talkin', you still like this worl'! Here's your jug, Sandy.

Sandy. That's it; draw up a cheer, Sam. Now, strangers, we're gittin' well 'quainted, h'aint we? You'll like the tavern! How's them flapjacks over thar by you?

Lucy. The very best I've ever eaten! Don't you think so, Agnes?

Agnes. They are certainly fine! Is it possible you made them, Sandy?

Sandy (*glowing with enthusiasm*). I make 'em? Let me tell you, flapjacks is considered the pride o' this tavern! aint they Sam?

Sam. Well, flapjacks is fust rate, but 'simmon beer's got the flavor!

Kent. It aint solid enough, Sam.

Sam. That's nothin', it's more digesterble. I'm in for digesterble things!

Lucy. It's a matter of taste, I think.

Sam. Right! Now there's the Parson, he's awful fond of hymn books and I aint; and I'm toler'ble fond of 'simmon beer, and he aint! that's all.

Sandy. Here's some hoe-cake, strangers, and a ten-pound loaf o' corn bread, won't you tackle it?

Lucy. Oh, my! I can't now.

Sandy. And here's some real old yam pertaters.

Sam. Yes, try them yams! I tell you, yams is gittin' scarce now-a-days. Take 'em when you can. I'm in for yam pertaters all the year roun': how's that, Parson?

Kent. Now I'm with you! Yes, sir, I'm in for yams and fried chicken!

Sam. That's so; chickens is gittin' scarce round here!

Kent. How's that?

Sam. I reckon it must be somethin' ailin' them, Parson. Eh, Sandy?

Sandy. I don't know, Sam; there's no tellin' what ——

Enter Philip Sly, in a tremendous rush.

Sly. Fight! fight! fight! I say.

All. Where?

Sly. Awful! tryin' to shoot each other down yonder—I'm jus' broke down! Some liquor, quick!

Sandy (*fetching a flask*). Who's shot? who's shot?

Lucy. Oh, Agnes, let's go!

Sly. You see, Bill Jones ——

Kent. Bill Jones! I thought so! —

Sly. You see, Bill Jones caught one o' Sam Kellum's oxen in his corn-patch and he shot it! Then Sam Kellum brings out his one bar'l gun and goes out to hunt Bill, but Bill was on the watch waitin' behind a tree—the big oak, you know—

Sandy. Go ahead! (*here Kent, greatly excited, makes for the scene of battle before he hears all the tale.*)

Sly And as Sam comes up, Bill knocks him flat, and the bloodiest fight! Even the niggers are jinin' in, and Aleck Fury, the Constable, wants help right off! That's what I'm here for! Somebody's killed!

Sandy. I'm off with you, old man! (*they rush out together, and Sam, picking up a billet of wood for a weapon, follows quickly.*)

Lucy. Agnes, I'm not going to stop here! We'll see it, too! (*Exeunt. In the excitement, Lucy drops her purse.*)

Enter Billy Sharp, with an old gripsack.

Sharp. Is them miserable critters gone? Ha! ha! ha! Phil's an awful sinner! Hello! what's in this jug? (*drinks.*) I don't know what it is—makes me smile all over (*sings*)!

I'm dusty and broke, forlorn and forsoke.
I walked, sir, from Colorado!
They call me a scamp, a rascally tramp!
Because I am hones' yer know!
Because I am hones', yer know!
I'm dusty and broke, forlorn and forsoke.
I walked, sir, from Colorado!

(Allows the head of a chicken to protrude from his pocket.)

(Sniffs odors from the table, and sits down.)

Hoe-cake! as I'm a sinner! Flapjacks! I tell you, it looks like old times! Let me taste this again (*drinks*). It gets me! I'll have to give up on that. It's got some ingredient in it I've never tasted before! (*While Sharp is thus absorbed in the midst *of his supper, Phil Sly, having slipped off from Sandy in the darkness, returns.)*

Enter Phil Sly in a rush.

Sharp (springing up). Jehosophat! You nearly made me swallow a pertater whole! How'd you git back so quick, Phil?

Sly. Well, Billy, I wanted a little fun myself! You see, I slunk away from them critters in the darkness. They was sittin' down, restin', not there yet.

Sharp. Oh, Phil, what a splendid chance! Let's eat!

Sly. You're right! (*sits down.*) Hello! what's this? (*Picks up Lucy's purse on the floor*).

Sharp. Oh, Phil, divide!—oh, yes now, Phil, divide! Give us half! You know, I forgot that part!

Sly. Billy, you forgits too much! It'll ruin you one of these days! Here's half and you may keep the purse.

Sharp. I don't want the purse; however, I'll chuck it in my gripsack; it'll do for a terbaccer bag, (*does so, and then goes behind Sandy's counter and opens his till*). Phil! Phil! (*jingling the coins.*)

Sly. My cup's runnin' over! Shake hands, Billy! Now let's walk round to the table and medertate! (*they sit down.*)

Sharp. Aint this comfortable, Phil? I like it.

Sly. It beats Colorado! Git out o' here! (*takes a chicken from his pocket and throws it upon the floor*) I'll put in some pertaters in place of raw chicken (*fills his pocket*).

Sharp. I say, Phil, 'spose we start for Texas to-morrow?

Sly. No sir, Billy! The fish are bitin' too well! You've got a splendid chance! Them people aint seen you yet!

Sharp. That's so! We'll work it!

Sly. I tell you, I'm jus' like everybody else, *I won't steal 'ceptin' I want ter!*

Sharp. So 'm I. So we'll lurk about here awhile longer! Well, sir, I'm in for it! I say, Phil, keep them taller candles you got; don't eat 'em, you hear? We'll want 'em!

Sly. Oh, yes, I've got 'em. (*At this point a ghastly expression comes over their countenances, as they hear a rapping at the door and music too. It is Warsaw, just arrived in his buggy. He raps upon the door with his fiddle-bow several times, and then plays the "Arkansas Traveller." Sly, after much running about, finally ensconces himself behind Sandy's counter, while Sharp is still looking for an exit.)*

Sharp (*rushing up the to counter*). Phil! Phil! come out o' there! You'll git caught!

Sly (*poking up his head*). No, sir! You can't git out anywhere! You'll git wound up!

Sharp. I'll risk it! (*Escapes with his gripsack through a small window.*)

Enter Hiram Warsaw, highly incensed at the delay; his carpetbag in his hand and his fiddle under his arm.

Warsaw. Perdition! Are you going to keep me out here all night? I've stood at that door until I'm colorblind! Hello! a chicken (*picks it up*), and nobody in! Is this a hen-coop? (*here the tramp rises in dismay, and, Warsaw's back being turned, creeps through the door.*) I'll see if I can't start the owner of this tavern (*tunes his fiddle and plays the "Ark. Trav."*)

Re-enter Phil Sly, pretending to be the tavern keeper.

Sly. Hello! stranger!

Warsaw. Hello! yourself! I was about to upset your tavern.

Sly. Well, you might have done it! You see, stranger, I was at the stable jus' now tendin' to a hoss, and you got in before I could git here. Hello! gimme that chicken you got there, he was sick and he died in here. Yes, gimme him, jes lemme have him and I'll save him for the cat—I will for a fact!

Warsaw. Apoplexy? I say, he gave in to apoplexy, didn't he?

Sly. Who?

Warsaw. The chicken, of course!

Sly. Oh! I dunno! I'm sorry that hoss kep' me so long. But you're hones', I see it by your look—What's your bizness, anyhow, stranger?

Warsaw. I was driving by in my buggy and thought I'd stop

over. What about the health of this place; any sickness?

Sly. Splendid place! People never die round here!

Warsaw (rising). Then I'll drive on to the next town. But it's rather late.

Sly. Well! Hol' on, stranger; what's your *perticler* line?

Warsaw. Any invalids here? Anybody dried up, shrivelled, warped? Anybody with the eyeache, earache, backache toothache—anything in that line, because I've got an infallible remedy—mark me—infalible—Warsaw's "Grip of Life," the Great Original, risk no other!

Sly. Bless your soul, stranger! bless your soul! I didn't know them's the kind you wanted! I nearly died with the backache myself last night, and most everybody's wrong somewhere! There is a few invalids, too. It's my opinyun—now I gives this from what I've seed—it's my opinyun, you can do a rousin' bizness!

Warsaw. Put me down for a week's board, you rusty old biped! (*goes over to the register on the counter behind which Sly has taken his stand; Warsaw registers.*) So that settles it, eh?

Sly. Yes, you're all right now, stranger, 'ceptin' one item—terms allus in advance! It's been my rule for twenty years, you see, to do a strict cash bizness and I hate to make 'ceptions. It's the best plan, and we'll close the bargain on ten dollars!

Warsaw. Oh! strictly cash? That's right! (*pulls out a roll of money, extends a ten-dollar bill, and, as Sly puts out his hand to take it, Warsaw suddenly withdraws it and scans the tramp carefully*) Well sir! you *are* the crudest looking old biped I ever saw! (*the tramp removes his hat to scratch his head*) Baldheaded, too! Perdition! bald as an orchestra!

Sly. I'se allus been so, stranger, allus!

Warsaw. Always?

Sly. Allus—born so!

Warsaw. Hold your head there a minute, old man! (*goes into his carpetbag for a bottle of his "Anti-Dandruff"*) Here's my "Anti-Dandruff"; now, hand me your head! I intend to rub some of it into it—warranted to make a baldhead bristle like a cocklebur Make haste!— You won't? Perdition! Then starve to death, that's all! Give me a receipt for that! (*flings over his ten-dollar bill.*) I never go without receipts—I have enough creditors on hand now! When a creditor hits my trail I lose my relish for this life! (*reads the receipt*) It's signed Sandy. Right! Now, old biped, walk right around here and take a seat by this table! Make haste! I'm going to tackle you! (*Warsaw sits down, and Sly, as he walks around, surveys him in dismay.*) How do you feel now?

Sly. Fustrate! fustrate! Splendid weather!

Warsaw (*tuning his fiddle*). I say, old man, just stand up there a minute, will you? Now walk right out to the front of me—a little to the right—there! You say you feel all right? (*the tramp nods assent*) Now, sir, I've just driven thirty-five miles to-day in my buggy, and I'm going to have some relaxation!—Get your legs ready! I'll start a tune, and you've got to dance the "Highland Fling!" Yes you do know it! It's dance or die! I tell you I want some recreation!—I'm ready! Now, strike an attitude! (*Sly hears noises outside and gets perturbed.*)

Sly. Jus' one minnit, stranger! I understan' it! Jus' wait till I lock my stable, I forgot it (*Exit*).

Warsaw. Hurry up, then! I'll saw your legs off if you don't! I'm going to have some fun in this tavern; I didn't come here to mope!

Enter Sandy, Sam, Kent, Lucy and Agnes—fatigued.

Sandy. Well, sir, the Big Fork Tavern's been fooled! Hello! stranger!

Warsaw. Hello! yourself! Sit down, old biped. I'm tuning up for a little fun (*becomes absorbed in tuning his fiddle*).

Sam. I'm going to finish what I started on (*sits down to the table and eats leisurely*). Hello! all them yams gone?

Sandy. They are? That's sing'ler (*scans Warsaw, who appears to hear nothing*). Some o' that hoe cake missin', too! And only one flapjack!

Lucy. Oh! Agnes, have you got your cushion?—Yes, I see it; that's right.

Kent. I wonder what that feller wanted to play sich a joke as that for? It don't strike me as bein' very nice to walk a mile and a half for nothin'!

Sandy. Nor I! I'd like to get hold o' him!

Lucy (*rushing up to Sandy*). Oh! Sandy! Sandy! My purse! my purse! It's gone!

Sandy (*in a whisper*). My stars! gone? Mebbe we are robbed! (*rushing to his till*) Robbed! How'd that come? Ha! (*pointing at Warsaw, who has just begun to play the "Ark. Trav."*) Sam! Parson! be ready! Thar's the man! (*goes towards Warsaw and slaps him upon the back*)

Warsaw. You abnormal gawk! Who are you? what do you want? where'd you come from and where are you going to? (*walks about excitedly*)

Sandy. Look here, stranger, it's no use your stannin' thar arguin' with me; you might's well own up and clar out! We're not goin' to give you much rope, neither! You can't git out of it! If you don't pull that money out mighty quick, we'll swing you to a tree! Gimme that rope yonder, Parson!

Warsaw. Be sure you're right, old gawk! You might get the worst of it. Read this! (*Sandy reads the receipt*) Given to me by an old baldheaded man in rusty clothes! (*sits down on Agnes's cushion which he gets hitched to his coat-tail*)

Sandy. What! It's the same feller! Friends, I see through it; we've been robbed by a rascally tramp!

Agnes. Oh! Lucy! We'll never see Kentucky! never!

Lucy. We'll wait here, Agnes! Just stand it!—Oh! where is that cushion? Did any one take it?

Kent. Not as I know of.

Warsaw (*stirred up, rises with the cushion dangling at his coat-tail*). Perdition! That unqualified rascal of a tramp's gone off with some of my money!

Lucy (*having bought a glimpse of the cushion*). My cushion, sir! Give me my cushion! You've got it! I saw it!

Warsaw (excited). Don't irritate me! Ridiculous! I have nt!

Agnes. You have, sir! You have! Oh! Lucy, let him alone, he's crazy!

Warsaw. Depart, you little junebug!

Sandy Grab him by the windpipe, Parson! He's got it! He's got it! Hold him! (*they rush at Warsaw—all except Sam, who is still at the table.*)

Warsaw. Back! back! you insufferable gawks! (*strikes an attitude of defiance and plays the "Ark. Trav.," while Kent manages to tap the cushion off with his stick*) Stop, sir! I'll stifle you!

Kent. Thar it is! I knowed you had it!

Warsaw (to Kent). You did it! (*to Sandy*) You did it! (*to Sam*) You did it! (*to Lucy and Agnes*) You girls did it!—Well, who did it? Nobody did it! It did itself! Of course it did! (*to Sandy*) I say, I'll get you to attend to my horse and buggy, out there, and now I want to go to bed! I want my room immediately!

Lucy. So do I!

Warsaw. No! you shant!

Lucy. I shall!

Warsaw. You shan't have my room!

Lucy. I don't wan't your room!

Warsaw. But you said you did!

Lucy. I did'nt!

Warsaw. You did!

Lucy. I didn't!

Warsaw. Well damn me! Who am I? (*strikes an attitude and plays the "Ark. Trav."*)

Sam. I'll stick to it, this is a tonic! It's nothin' else!

Sandy. Here's the number to your room, stranger. It's number two—number one belongs to them ladies. And now all's ready, if you want to go.

Warsaw (who has gotten his carpetbag ready to depart). Are you sure you're right, old man?

Sandy. Oh! yes; it's number two, stranger!

Warsaw. I merely ask to know for certain. Don't get me mixed with this other party, understand? There'll be a collision! (*Warsaw advances toward the front of the stage, with his carpetbag*) Goodnight! Which way'll I go? (*here Lucy, thinking the carpetbag is hers from its close resemblance, hurriedly makes toward Warsaw and grasps his arm*) Madam! what game are you playing now?*

Lucy. I'm not playing any game!

Warsaw. You are! You've tried to irritate my nervous system!

Agnes (*advancing*). Oh! Lucy, he's insane!

Lucy. I haven't!

Warsaw. You have! Youv've singled me out for your venom from the first!

Lucy. I havn't!

Warsaw. Provoking woman! you have! you've been at right-angles with me all night!

Lucy. I haven't at all, sir!

Warsaw. You have, madam! I'm bristling all over!

Lucy. I tell you plainly, you are going off with my property sir!

Warsaw. Uncalled for nonsense!

Lucy. That carpetbag is mine, sir! It's mine!

Warsaw. Delusive dream!

Lucy. I know it! I know my property!

Warsaw. Madam!—mark me—I've been here fifteen minutes and cleaned out the till, stolen your purse, gone off with that abominable cushion, and now I am positively accused of stealing my own carpetbag!

Lucy. Oh! Sandy! Sandy! come here!

Sandy (*rushing up*). Gimme me the key! gimme the key! We'll settle it! (*Warsaw gives his key*)

Lucy. It's mine! it's mine! I said so! I said so! (*Sandy opens, and tosses a deck of cards upon the floor.*)

Warsaw (*instantaneously*). Yours, madam! yours! I beg your pardon! (*strides off in triumph*)

---

*This incident is founded upon a fact. It is mine in part only.

Lucy (*completely undone, gazes at the cards a moment*). You villain! you villain!

[CURTAIN.]

NOTE—The following positions seem to me to be the most effective: Warsaw's fiddle is held under his left arm; his left hand is tipping his hat apologetically to Lucy, while his extended right hand is meekly accepted by her. Just behind, Samuel Easy is standing serenely puffing his pipe. as if he had already known exactly how the affair must turn out.

ACT II.

—o::o—

SCENE—*Interior of Warsaw's room Morning. Lucy appears at the door, and, having assured herself, enters cautiously.*

Lucy. Well! he's out! I wonder where he is! Just the thing! I haven't much curiosity, but I'm determined to explore this tavern all over, now that I must remain here for awhile. My! if he were to catch me in here! what should I do? Ugh! what's that? a roach! There! he's gone! I never could kill one. Mercy! who was that? I think I had better be going. (*goes to the door cautiously in such a way that, as Warsaw pushes it open suddenly, she is shut behind it.*)

Enter Warsaw.

Warsaw (*opening his carpetbag*). Come to business at last! I've just made a tour of this place. My heavens! the amount of dandruff in this town! it is perfectly amazing! Let's see, I want a bottle of the "Grip" and one of the "Anti-Dandruff" for the constable —Perdition! I thought that door was open! There's an awful draught! (*slams the door*) Cæsar! stop, Lucy! stop! stand your ground! never mind!

Lucy. Oh! horrors!

Warsaw. Why, Lucy, ain't you tamed yet?

Lucy. No! I'm not! You say so, because my wing is clipped!

Warsaw. Well—I've seen ducks with a broken wing fairly travelling over the water! how's that?

Lucy. Was I going fast?

Warsaw. Just so, so. Come here now, let me tame you!—confound that roach!

Lucy. It's the very one I tried to kill!

Warsaw. Lucy, mark me, a tavern-roach can't be killed any more'n an Indian chief. Now last night I was about to fall off into into an ordinary doze when something began to scratch at the bottom of the bedpost. The party, thus occupied, pushed himself up a little till he got on a level with me; then he halted and thought. Presently he started again, having concluded not to interview me. I heard him drag himself up to the very top. There he sat and sat, and thought and thought; then he became alarmed, got dizzy and began to whirl around on his pivot—delirious, you see. Presently he toppled over and struck the floor with a thud! He did it all himself!

Lucy. Horrible fib!—Where were you awhile ago?

Warsaw. I was making a tour of the town. Although the woods are pretty heavy about here, still I find a good many people scattered around. It is amazing the amount of dandruff about here!—Here, Lucy, just taste this!

Lucy. No, no, no; I don't want any of your "Anti-Dandruff!"

Warsaw. This isn't the "Anti-Dandruff."

Lucy. It isn't?

Warsaw. No! it's the "Grip of Life," warranted to resuscitate a mummy! Risk no other!

Lucy. Well, I don't believe I care for any.

Warsaw. Three drops to a pint of water, that's amply sufficient, eh?

Lucy. No, let me off this time!

Warsaw. You'd better; mark me, it'll fix you to a moral certainty!

Lucy. No! I will not take it!

Warsaw. Provoking girl, how can I rescue you?

Lucy. I won't touch it!

Warsaw. That settles it! A won't is a won't; women do just what they want! Yes, sir, women can do anything except whistle two tunes at the same time! They'll have to give up on that, there's no use talking!

Lucy. What, are you going?

Warsaw. Yes, Lucy, the constable is waiting for these bottles now! But won't you wait till I come back?

Lucy. No, I must go and find Agnes.

Warsaw. Won't you come back after a while then?

Lucy. Yes, I will!

Warsaw. Don't forget it! (*Exit*).

Lucy. What a queer fellow! So I'm I! Two queer fellows—he—I—How funny! (*goes to the door in such a manner that, as Kent pushes it open suddenly, she is again shut behind it. I will here observe that, in order to execute this act properly, Warsaw's room must be arranged with two doors at the back part, standing opposite to each other.*)

Enter Hezekiel Kent.

Kent. I'll take three bottles! Hey, the Trav'ler's out! However, I'll wait for him. I had a chill last night and ached all over. I tell you, I'm shaking all over now! It's toler'ble chilly in here! No wonder! just look at that door wide open! (*shuts it*) Hallelujah! who's that?

Lucy. Stop, Parson! stop! Stand your ground!

Kent. Dear me! I thought you were Sam; he told me he was comin' here to git a bottle. Are you in a scrape, too?

Lucy. Yes—I caught you, and somebody caught me!

Kent. Is that the way?

Lucy. Yes, that's it!

Kent. Ha! ha! ha! lemme put you down for my congergation!

Lucy. No, no, no.

Kent. Why not?

Lucy. I don't want to; I'm only going to stay here till I hear from home.

Kent. Oh! yes; that's so.

Lucy. I'm afraid of Parsons anyhow; (*drops her handkerchief and picks it up quickly; the Parson reaches for it, too, just too late, and feels uncomfortable*)

Kent (*uncomfortable*), Well—well, I'm sorry you won't Have a seat anyhow, won't you? (*sits down upon his hat*) Oh! me, why did I do that?

Lucy. I can't tell you.

Kent. I tell you, I'm not well; I'm awtul chilly!

Lucy. That's it! Of course it is!—

Agnes (*appearing at the door*) Lucy! Lucy! what are you doing in there? (*exit Lucy through one door; away goes Kent to the other, where he stumbles into the arms of Sam Easy, who has just come "for a bottle"*

Enter Sam Easy, dragging the Parson.

Sam. Come back here! It's no use to fool me! Confess your sins, Parson!

Kent. Now, Sam, ever since the other night, the tavern's been out of order; you know that yourself—

Sam. Yes.

Kent. And everybody's been plunged into a scrape!

Sam. And you've been tryin' to git out of one! It's human natur'.

Kent. That's so; things aint been runnin' exactly smooth around here!

Sam. Far as I could see, you were goin' along toler'ble smooth! You're a parson, I know, but you've got your weak points.

Kent. That's true; there was nothin' wrong, Sam; I was only waitin' for the Trav'ler. Have you seen him?

Sam. He'll be along d'rectly. He was doin' some loud talkin' down yonder.

Kent. Yes, he'll make some money; I wish he'd jine my congergation!

Sam. Somebody's comin' now.

Enter Warsaw, considerably ruffled about something; quickly pushes a box against the door and props a chair against it. Then he describes a circle around Sam and Kent.

Warsaw. Perdition! That fellow shan't come into my room! No sir! he shall not! He will actually ruin my business!

Sam. Who?

Warsaw. That unparalleled idiot, Jake Brown!

Kent. What, old Jake who's got the wooden leg?

Warsaw. Yes, sir, the demon with the cork leg!

Sam. Old Jake never did have much sense; but what's he up to?

Warsaw. I can't get rid of him! You see, I was out yonder making a speech to that gaping crowd, and working a few miracles, when old Jake walked up smiling all over with delight, and beckoned to me with his finger. He's got the notion that I can start a new leg for him—a fresh one, you see—as if I could supply the country with legs!

Kent. Curious, aint it? Is he comin' up here?

Warsaw. He said he'd drop in here directly. I'll get ugly if he does. (*goes into his carpetbag for his flask.*)

Sam. That's the trouble with Jake; he's good-hearted, but when he gits a notion in his head, it's got to work its way through.

Warsaw. Now, boys, this is one of my odd times; take a little out of this flask, Parson!

Kent. Really, it's agin' my principles!

Sam. Yes, I'll take some; my throat's as husky as a corn cob in June! (*drinks*) Thar's old Jake now, hammerin' at your door! Just wait; I'll go out there and talk to him a bit (*exit*).

Warsaw. Go ahead then! You see, Parson, he will hurt my business—Really you do look badly; now let me persuade you, as a gentleman, to take a little out of this flask. Now I ask you as a gentleman; it'll help you.

Kent. Now I agree with you! You see, Trav'ler, my great object has been to set that feller Sam a good example to incutate, and now, havin' done everything in my power to rescue him from everlastin' ruin, I say—

Warsaw. Oh! perdition! Drink, man! It won't hurt you!

Kent. Well I will, notwithstandin' I'm a parson. (*drinks*)

Enter Sam.

Sam (*to Jake outside*). Go home, Jake!—How's it taste, Parson!

Kent. Why don't you go home! You're everywhere at the same time! Why don't you go and tote wood, or use an axe, or split rails sometimes, eh?

Sam. If you'll only take my advice, Parson—

Kent. I don't want it! I'll go home, that's all! I'm perfectly disgusted with you! (*exit*)

Sam. Now he's riled at me because he sold out cheap!

Warsaw. That's so! The devil buys at auction!—Where'd you leave old Jake?

Sam. Well, he says he knows you *can* do somethin' for him! He's out there.

Warsaw. I can stifle him! (*takes a package from his carpetbag*)

Sam. What's that you've got in your hand?

Warsaw. That's a pack of testimonials. Just hold them awhile.

Sam. And what's them bright-lookin' things?

Warsaw. They're only medals. Hold them while I go a little deeper into this carpetbag.

Sam. These look nice.—There's old Jake again! (*Goes to the door*) Go home, Jake! clar out from here!

Warsaw. Let him hammer, if he wants! Ah! here's what I've been looking for! (*draws out his shaving set*)

Sam. What's that?

Warsaw. It's my shaving set. I'm going to take a shave. I do so every day. (*makes his preparatioas*)

Sam. I say, Trav'ler, you've succeeded toler'ble well, haven't you?

Warsaw. Pretty well, Sam.

Sam. That's what I've always said; all a man wants is brains, just brains, and if he'll only take my advice, he'll succeed!

Warsaw. How's that?

Sam. All a man's got to do to make a livin' is to go straight ahead on a dead level—understan'?

Warsaw. Exactly. That reminds me—

Sam. But wait; after you've gone ahead about ten years and have larned how to use figgers well—but you're not listenin'!

Warsaw. Yes I am. Go on; that wasn't anything; I just thought it was a roach crawling up my pants leg.

Sam. When you've spent ten years thuswise, what are you goin' to do with the money you've made? Now lemme tell you somethin'—I say, aint you been laughin' at me?

Warsaw. Perdition, man! I feel as if my grand-mother had just died! Go on!

Sam. Hold to your money yourself! For I tell you, money's as hard to hold on to as a fresh water eel!

Warsaw. That's so, it's awful slippery! (*brings the tavern mirror into full view, in order to scan his countenance. This mirror is cracked in all directions.*)

Sam. And have nothin' to do with State bon's, nothin' on earth! There's no tellin' when them bon's is goin' to shrivel up like a pair o' wet shoes before a blazin' fire!

Warsaw (*viewing himself in the mirror*). Oh! I'll have to give up on this!—Go on, Sam, go on! I was only blocked.

Sam. My head's solid now; didn't use to be. You know, I once managed a farm and wurked like a pile-driver for awhile, and aint done much since. But, sir, the time come when that farm got upside down, went all to pieces, and to save my life, I couldn't keep a hen on the nest!

Warsaw. And so you got married?

Sam. I confess it!—I tell you, it's no easy thing gittin' rich these days; a feller can't git rich to save his life—too many banks!

Warsaw. You're right, Sam! Putting your money into banks is like going to church: you wake up after it's all over!

Sam. I was on the p'int of sayin' that myself—There's that doleful critter agin! Jake! why can't you go home? What'll we do with that everlastin' fool?

Warsaw. Positively this is his last chance! I shall mangle him beyond recognition! How's that, Sam?

Sam. No. he's lame, Trav'ler; let's try somethin' else!

Warsaw. What then—some insidious drug?

Sam. No, anythin' that'll scare him to death and won't hurt him.

Warsaw. Come here then, I've got something tip-top!

Sam. What is it? what is it?

Warsaw. All you have to do is to take your stand on this side the door, and I'll plant myself on the other side—

Sam. Then what?

Warsaw. Then you'll draw the chair and the box aside, and just as he crosses the threshold, I'll fresco his countenance with my lather-brush!

Sam. Ha! ha! ha! magnificient! I'll go into spasms! (*drinks*)

Warsaw. Then we'll tell him he's got hydrophobia! Come on, quick!

Sam. Oh! Lord, aint that splendid?—Here goes the box, Trav'ler! Hey, lemme have your beaver hat, won't you? Old Jake knows me, and I wouldn't like to be found out! (*puts on Warsaw's beaver*) Now, sir, keep your nerves steady!

Warsaw (*grinning all over*). The finest thing ever thought of! Just wait a moment, Sam, let me get a good souse of lather! There! now drag them!

Sam. All's ready!

Warsaw. Come in! Persistent demon, enter! Individual with the cork leg, come in, I say!—Ah-h-h-h!

Enter Lucy, who receives the lather

Sam (*thrusting the beaver down over his head to escape recognition*). Hallelujah!

Warsaw. Perdition! I've lost my identity!

Lucy (*dumbfounded*). Wretch! didn't you ask me to return! Sandy! Sandy! (*exit*)

Enter Sandy.

Sandy. Ha! you're caught at last! (*Warsaw, flinging off his outer garment, displays a plaster, whereon is printed—Warsaw's Grip. Risk no other! He strikes an attitude of defiance and plays the "Arkansas Traveller."*

[CURTAIN.]

ACT III.

—o: :o—

SCENE—*Interior of the Big Fork Tavern. Morning. Warsaw sitting at table at the conclusion of breakfast. Tuning his fiddle. His carpetbag near by.*

Enter Sandy.

Sandy. Well, stranger, have you finished?

Warsaw. Yes, sir, take off your dishes.

Sandy. Thar's somethin' new in town this mornin'.

Warsaw. What's that, old man?

Sandy. It's a sorter circus—got here early.

Warsaw. A country circus, eh? I've got to go down that way directly; I'll see.

Sandy. I oughter git one or two boarders by it.

Warsaw. No doubt you will.

Sandy. Oh! thar's plenty room! The tavern's been fixed up to 'commerdate a good many! (*exit, with the dishes*)

Warsaw. You can accommodate a good many roaches. I caught one last night, and fiddled him to death! (*strikes up the "Ark. Trav."*)

Enter Agnes, languid.

Agnes. Oh! my, I'm so tired of this! Such trouble and vexation!

Warsaw. What, trouble? Sit down, little girl, and let me tell you how long *I've* been chewing the cud of vexation.

Agnes. You? the idea! Just think of it!

Warsaw. Yes, think of it! Why, I've been pursued by evil spirits for years! Mark me, ill-luck is my destiny! Now Agnes, give me your ears a minute! I first started in the sewing-machine business—an agent for a large house. It is needless to remark that I got along finely, until the house failed. Then I quit the business. I won't work for a bankrupt house; I won't make myself sick for anybody, because when I once get sick, I've got to diet myself on gravy for a month! I'm very particular. After this failure, I began to sell a cement, the finest on earth! It held on to anything and to everything it got hold of. I'll give you an idea: I happened to be at a railroad depot one day when I saw two trains, filled with passengers, backing up against each other. I playfully added a little of this cement to the coupling, you know, and when they struck together, it was found impossible to get them apart. I took my seat upon a doorstep and watched results. At last, however, I had to leave, for it was a hot summer day and the profanity became so loud and appalling, as to bring down the value of real estate along there. As I was leaving, an old miner approached and separated them with a pickaxe. The company sued me for damages, and I was wrecked again!

Agnes. What did you do after that?

Warsaw. My next freak was a peculiar one. I entered into what is known as the tombstone business—selling tombstones, or headstones, to people that wanted them. I sold seven to one woman, who was then laying her snare for her eighth husband. I expect she got him. I was an agent for the tomb, you see; I used to go as far as the grave with people, but no further—it's hot enough on this side. Now Agnes, the time to go into the tombstone business is in spring; I hit it in May. Easterly winds were blowing, indigestion was rife, and everybody was committing suicide. For a few weeks I reaped a harvest, but suddenly the bottom flew out of everything. I told you, ill-luck's my destiny. If it had been some other fellow, success would have constantly rewarded him; *but just because I was in the tombstone business making a living, then everybody stopped dying.* The whole country got healthy. And the ugly part of it is this: Three ravenous doctors and three pale undertakers formed themselves into a double-barreled committee and intimated to me, that unless I changed my occupation double-quick, my corpse would be necessary to their happiness! Wasn't that a ghastly request?

Agnes (*rising to go*). It was; and then what did you do?

Warsaw. Then I became proprietor of the "Anti-Dandruff" and the "Grip of Life," the Great Original, risk no other!

Agnes. Well, I must go and find Lucy; she was writing a letter.

Warsaw. Tell her to come down here and write; I'm awful fond of letter-writing myself!

Agnes (*at the door*). Dear me, what a queer-looking man coming here? Perhaps he wants board. (*exit*)

Enter Billy Sharp, with his gripsack—regards Warsaw carefully.

Warsaw (*beckoning*). Hey, come here, old gawk! Sit down! You want board, eh?

Sharp Exactly, stranger. You see, I belong to the circus what's just come in.

Warsaw. Oh! you do? Then you're a clown! Crack two or three jokes for us, won't you?

Sharp. No, no, I'm sorter gin'ral manager.

Warsaw. You say you are the menagerie?

Sharp. No! 'course not! Manager, man!

Warsaw. Oh! perdition, I thought you were the menagerie! Who is then?

Sharp. Nobody is!

Warsaw. Point blank now, you won't crack a joke for us? (*the tramp shakes his head*) Give us something else then! Here now, let's see you knit your brows, contract them, I mean, so as to drag your ears around over your eyes, let's see you do it!

Sharp. This ain't the time to be doin' them things!

Warsaw. That's nothing! Then try this: Let's see you take

your left leg and put it around over the back of your neck—understand?—then I'll grab you by the right leg down near the ankle, and I'll whirl you around like a flying dutchman! Let's see you do it!

Sharp. By dad, I won't do it!

Warsaw. Amazing! why can't you afford a man some recreation! A nice clown! Then I'll go: I've got to make a speech to that gaping crowd! There's Sandy now. (*exit, with fiddle and carpetbag.*

Enter Sandy.

Sandy. Is it board you want, stranger?

Sharp. Yes, I'll stop a day or two with you; I belong to the circus.

Sandy. That's what I thought; lemme put your bag behin' the counter here. (*does so*)

Sharp. Thanks; yes, we're jus' in from the Upper Arkansas. It's a fine country, but full of rogues. By the way, who's that feller in here with the fiddle and the carpetbag? Ain't he from the Upper Arkansas, too?

Sandy. Yes, I believe he is.

Sharp. I thought so; ain't he sollin' some sorter medicine for the hair?

Sandy. Yes, he is; why?

Sharp. And his name is Warsaw?

Sandy. That's it. What's the matter?

Sharp. I know him! A hint's enough!

Sandy. What!

Sharp. Keep your eye on him! He's equal to a coon! Well-known fifty miles above here!

Sandy. Well sir, I've suspicioned him from the very first night! I'll watch him close!

Sharp. That's all you've got to do, and keep mum; I'll tell you what I know about *him* after awhile. Now I'm going on down to the circus (*goes toward the door on the pretense of going out*); so I wish you'd git my room ready right off, if you please.

Sandy. I will, this very minnit, stranger (*exit, through the door behind the counter. Having got rid of Sandy, the tramp reconnoitres, picks up Warsaw's handkerchief under the table; then goes to the door, and perceiving Kent coming, defers his design for a time.*)

Enter Hezekiel Kent.

Sharp. Come and set down, stranger; you look tired. 'Been walkin'?

Kent. Yes, a good deal. I thought I'd stop and take a rest. How are you feelin'?

Sharp. Putty well. What's your name?

Kent. Hezekiel Kent's my name.

Sharp. And what bizness are you doin' now?

Kent. I'm a circuit-rider.

Sharp. A circus-rider? Well sir! I'm glad to hear that!

Kent. You are? Why's that?

Sharp. Why, I'm a circus-rider myself!

Kent (*delighted*). Is it possible you are a circuit-rider? What's your name?

Sharp. My name is Sharp.—A circus-rider, well sir!

Kent (*rising*). Brother Sharp! how are you? (*the Parson shakes his hand vigorously, to the astonishment of the tramp. They then sit down*).

Sharp. That's sorter sing'ler.

Kent. It is mighty sing'ler! Yes, sir, it is sing'ler.

Sharp. Lemme your knife a minnit, won't you, to cut a piece of terbaccer?

Kent. With pleasure, Brother Sharp! (*does so*) I'm glad I stepped in; I had been visitin' some o' my people.—Sam Kellum was putty sick two hours ago.

Sharp. Sam Kellum? I'm jus' from town myself and somebody told me he was dyin' fast!

Kent (*rising quickly*). Dyin'? Is that so? Excuse me, Brother Sharp! (*rushes forth immediately*)

Sharp (*reflecting*). What the devil's the matter with that man?—Brother Sharp, how are you? By dad, he ain't no kin to me! No, sir! (*puts Kent knife into his pocket, then taps Sandy's till and deposits Warsaw's handkerchief by way of circumstantial evidence. Afterwards he saunters forth from the tavern and presently returns, having met Aleck Fury, the Constable.*)

Enter Aleck Fury and Billy Sharp.

Aleck. So you found the tavern? I've jus' come to see.

Sharp. Yes, you put me on the right road. It's a fine tavern.

Aleck Oh! it is; fustrate! Here's Sandy, now.

Enter Sandy, through the door behind the counter.

Sandy. Well, Aleck!

Aleck. Hey, Sandy, I sent you this guest; he come here accordin' to my advice. I'll serve you a good turn whenever I can, Sandy.

Sandy. You always do, Aleck.

Sharp. Yes, he did recommen' me to come here, seein' that I was a stranger. Now let's all go up to my room, come on!

Aleck. No, no, I must be back!—Bizness—bizness—bizness! (*exit*)

Sandy. Well, sir, it's ready, and I'll show you up to it. Let's walk easy, because them ladies are asleep up stairs. (*they make for the door behind the counter, and Sandy, seeing the handkerchief, picks it up.*)

Sharp. What is that you've got?

Sandy. It's a handkerchief; wonder whose it is?

Sharp. Ain't it got a name on the corner?—Yes, thar it is?

Sandy. Let's see—War-saw—My stars! (*examining his till*) Robbed again!

Sharp. Robbed! run for the constable quick! (*rushes to the door*)

Sandy. Stop! stop! say nothin'! We'll catch him ourselves?

Sharp. Let's choke the rascal! I can see him comin' away off yonder now. Yes, it's him.

Sandy. Then let's keep close! keep mum! We'll bait him for certain!

Sharp. Bait him, that's the thing! Come on right straight to my room and I'll help you to fix a plan! Bait the rascal!

Sandy. Gimme your hand on that, won't you? Come on quick! (*they shake hands and go out*)

Enter Warsaw and Sam Easy.

Warsaw. So you went down to see the circus, Sam?

Sam. Yes, I did; I'm perfectly disgusted - saw old Jake Brown there.

Warsaw. You did? Let him keep out of my clutches, that's all. Hello! where's that old gawk anyhow? Maybe he's gone!

Sam. Is he?

Warsaw. No, there's his old carpetbag behind the counter.

Sam. It is? Oh! let's have a little fun out of it; jus' look at it for fun.

Warsaw. No, you'd better not molest it, Sandy might not like it, Sam.

Sam (*going behind the counter*). That's nothin', I'll not hurt it; Sandy knows me. Jerusalem! it's heavy! feel it.

Warsaw (*shaking it vigorously*). Great Cæsar! it must be full of solid gold. There! it's come open! Perdition, Sam, just look at the hay, will you!

Sam. Hay? my lord, look at it!

Warsaw. Brickbats, too; just look at 'em! (*takes some out*)

Sam. His circus ain't nowhere, man. But what's the pherloserphy of it, anyhow?

Warsaw. Mark me, he's got some game on hand; he's filled his gripsack with hay and brickbats to give it size and weight. Then he put it behind the counter here as a kind of security, to ward off suspicion, and when he's gotten through with his job, he's going to leave without paying his board.

Sam. That's it; now for Sandy!

Warsaw. No, sir! come back! Let me have charge of this case, and I'll work that old gawk like a ripsaw; we'll have some recreation out of this; yes, sir, we'll do it to-night! Now, Sam, while I put this bag back behind the counter, just take my fiddle and carpetbag and wait for me in my room, won't you? We'll settle on a plan for to-night.

Sam. All right; here goes! (*exit*)

Warsaw. Let's see; I'll dive a little deeper into this bag just to find out a little more—a brick—another brick—some hay and sand—another brick—hey, here's something else, away down at the bottom- what is it—perdition, a pocket-book! The rascal! what does he want with a pocket-book? He may keep the bricks and I'll keep the purse and show it to Sam. (*puts it into his side pocket*) Now I'll put this bag back into the exact spot—let's see, I'm in a fix myself (*while he is trying to put the gripsack into the same place behind the counter, Lucy enters without his knowledge*).

Enter Lucy, a little sleepy, holding a half-written letter in her hand—sits down at the table to write. Presently Warsaw, exasperated at something, springs to his feet and hurls his bearer across the room).

Warsaw (*to his bearer*). Perdition! get out of my way!

Lucy. Oh! horrors! who is that? (*drops her letter*)

Warsaw. Be calm, excited girl! that hat's at the bottom of it. I tell you, as fast as I pushed it back on my head, it would slip down again over my eyes, till I became abnormal!

Lucy. Yes, but what are you doing behind that counter? Explain that.

Warsaw. I'll tell you everything directly, Lucy; I'm preparing for a little episode in the history of the Big Fool Tavern.—Hello! so you've heard from home? (*picks up Lucy's letter*)

Lucy. No, I was writing a letter; I expect to hear this evening.

Warsaw. Then you'll leave in the morning?

Lucy. In the morning, if I hear.

Warsaw. Then I'll go, too! (*reads*)

Lucy. Stop! give me my letter!

Warsaw. Oh! no, Lucy, let me read it.

Lucy. No, no, no, I don't want to.

Warsaw. Why? I'd let you.—Oho! I understand!

Lucy (*suspicious*). What now?

Warsaw. You are writing to some other fellow, that's it!

Lucy. Why, Hiram! I'm not at all! Then read it! It's more than you would do!

Warsaw. It isn't Lucy! (*reads with satisfaction*) Oh! this is your acknowledgement, is it? Then, Lucy, none but you and me shall know it yet!

Lucy. Now isn't that more than you would do? *You* wouldn't permit any one to rear *your* letters.

Warsaw. Why, Lucy, I'd let you—

Lucy. You will? - Then I'll put you to the test, sir! It isn't in the nature of a man to do so!

Warsaw. How ignorant you are of men!

Lucy. Come here now (*pulls him aside*); let me have this letter I see in your pocket. (*takes it out herself*)

Warsaw. That's from a friend of mine, a former clerk in a big dry goods house. Afterwards, he became a runner—he's a runner still!

Lucy. Where is he?

Warsaw. Rusticating in the south of France! He wants to know if it's time to come home; I told him to take it quietly for ten years more.

Lucy (*pulling out a travelling flask from anothe· pocket*). And what is this?

Warsaw. Oh! Lucy, don't touch that!

Lucy. Why, what is it?

Warsaw. It's nothing but medicine—cures snake-bites!

Lucy. Oh! yes, I know it does! How much you must suffer!

Warsaw. In my business, Lucy, a man must go armed with antidotes.

Lucy. And how often are you snake-bitten? (*returns the flask*)

Warsaw. It's chronic with me!

Lucy. Well, here is another letter. How many have you?

Warsaw. No, that is a song of mine, a poem called "My Percussion Cap;" I'll sing it for you after awhile

Lucy. You will? I'll be sure to remind you of it; here it is.

Warsaw (*reading it over and commenting upon it somewhat abstractedly*). I wrote this thing myself; consequently it's good. The metre is astonishingly fine and the cadences are just like rolling down a hill. (*here Lucy discovers the purse in his side pocket, and moves away without his knowledge*) When I have laid my snare for to-night—by the way (*turning*)—Oh, Lucy, how have I pained you! Lucy! Lucy!

Lucy (*to Agnes, just entering*). Oh! Agnes! Agnes! my purse!

Agnes. Who had it, sister?

Lucy (*turning toward Warsaw*). No!—I will not speak it!

Warsaw. Not I, Lucy, not I!

[CURTAIN.]

ACT IV.

—o: :o—

SCENE—*Interior of the Big Fork Tavern. Night of the same day, Sandy standing behind the counter and Sharp sitting at table. conversing. Midnight. Morning.*

Sharp. Well, we've got it all fixed now. How much was it you lost this morning?

Sandy. I los' ten dollars out o' the till—putty good sum.

Sharp. Yes, it is. How much did you put in thar jus' now to bait him with?

Sandy. Five dollars; I didn't want to risk too much, you see.

Sharp. Well yes; but 'spose you add this dollar o' mine to make it more temptin'; we must hook him in for certain.

Sandy. Well I will, if you've got no objection (*does so*).

Sharp. We are putty certain that feller Sam Easy aint got a hand in it, too.

Sandy. Lord, no; I've known Sam for many a year, and it

aint them ladies, of course. It's that feller sellin' the medicine, he's the man.

Sharp. We've got the inside track, and so let's hol' to the clue! I say, d'rectly we'll go out and take a walk down toward the circus jus' to give him a chance. We might get him.

Sandy. Yes, we'll stay out about an hour—Hush! I hear somebody comin' now.

Sharp. Then let's go ter'ble soon.

Enter Warsaw and Lucy.

Sandy. Come in, strangers; I've got an appintment to go down to the village for awhile, and I'll have to leave you.

Lucy. Don't let us detain you, then.

Sharp. I believe I'll go with you, Sandy, it's such a nice walk (*exeunt*).

Warsaw (*aside*). We'll walk you off to jail after awhile.

Lucy. Oh! Hiram, why don't you let me tell Sandy that the man's nothing but a tramp?

Warsaw. No, no, Lucy; if you do, the fellow might get away, and you'll ruin my plan. I've got charge of this case, and the plan is all fixed.

Lucy. It is? what is it?

Warsaw. I want to show Sandy that he's been suspecting the wrong man, and I'll open his eyes. We must go slowly, you see. Now I've let the constable, Aleck Fury, into the secret, and he's in for a little recreation himself. After awhile, about midnight, I'll station him outside the door there, and then Sam and myself will embrace the biped.

Lucy. Oh! then that's just the thing.

Warsaw. And we'll find out how he got hold of the purse, for it is evident he has a partner.

Lucy. It's that old bald-headed tramp. I can see him now. (*gaping*). My! my! my! I'm so tired!

Warsaw. My goodness! you're not angry with me, are you?

Lucy. No!

Warsaw. Then don't throw me off my guard so suddenly;

you almost take the cake, Lucy. But let me tell you, I'm acquainted with a woman on the Upper Arkansas, who, in the matter of yawning, has no parallel in the history of this country - none whatever! Mark me, when that woman has talked herself into a relaxed condition, and then has eaten a dinner sufficient for a Baptist conference, there was no such thing as measuring the extensiveness of one of her yawns—

Lucy. Oh! nonsense—That hasn't anything to do with this matter!

Warsaw. Positively, Lucy, I have seen that woman yawn until her ears slipped around into her mouth and disappeared! Now that looks like exaggeration, don't it?

Lucy (*highly indignant*). It's false, sir; I do not believe any such thing!

Warsaw. You don't!

Lucy. No, sir! I do not—absurd! Do you think I would believe that?

Warsaw. Lucy! nothing is impossible to women!

Lucy. Now stop right there! If pou are going to quarrel with me at the beginning, then what?

Warsaw. Then we'll have to make up right off, Lucy. Although facts are stubborn things, they must give way. There! (*extending his hand*) Now you won't irritate me any more, will you?

Lucy. Agreed—I will not!

Warsaw. That's a girl! —Well, here's Sam.

Enter Samuel Easy, with an anxious countenance. Smokes vigorously and keeps on the alert. Presently Agnes rushes in from another quarter and Sam begins to retreat.

Agnes. Stop, sir! stop, I say! Wasn't that you, sir?

Warsaw. What's the matter now?

Agnes. Wait; let him answer me! Didn't you come rushing into my room just now?

Sam. Well, hol' on—

Lucy. I expect it was a mistake, Agnes.

Warsaw. That's evident.

Sam. It was; you see, Trav'ler, I was comin' along to see you about that bizness, an' it bein' very dark upstairs, I got in the wrong room and walked up to the bed where I thought I seed you an'—

Agnes. Yes, you puffed some of your vile tobacco smoke all over my head! I'll never get rid of it! Now I'll forgive you this time, sir.

Warsaw. That settles it then; she forgives you, Sam. How's that?

Sam. Oh! that's all right- Well, I 'spose you're goin' to 'tend to that feller about midnight?

Warsaw. Yes, it's getting late now. You had better take a little rest, Lucy.

Lucy. Yes, I am; come on, Agnes, I'm very tired. We're going to leave in a few hours, you know.

Sam (*casting a leer at Agnes*). Yes, a nap'll do you good; I'm goin' to take a snooze myself d'rectly. (*exeunt Lucy and Agnes*)—Is everything ready?

Warsaw. I've got Aleck ready, but it isn't time yet.

Sam. Oh! no; but I tell you what I'm goin' to do, Trav'ler; I'm goin' behin' that counter and take Sandy's money out 'o that till I've jus' thought of it; that disgustin' tramp will steal it!

Warsaw. Right! it hadn't occurred to me.

Sam. Six dollars, exactly. You take charge of it, because I'm goin' to take a nap in Sandy's room. Losin' sleep kills me out, sir

Warsaw. Well, you have'nt long to take a nap, Sam. Look here, don't oversleep yourself.

Sam. No, no, I'm the last man in the worl' to do that! I'l be here to the very dot (*exit*).

Warsaw. It's time for those fellows to be back; let me take a look. I believe they are coming now. I'll wait for them anyhow. Here's somebody coming.

Enter Sandy and Sharp.

Sandy. Well, we've been gone a good time, hain't we?

Sharp. Longer'n we thought.

Warsaw. It's a fine night, though, and you don't mind walking anyhow, do you?

Sharp. I walk mighty little. I can't git used to it, Sandy

Sandy. That's the way with some people; it goes hard with 'em.--By the way, I wonder if my stable's locked? Wait here a bit won't you? (*exit*)

Sharp. That's the safest way, lock things up.—I say, stranger, let's have a little quiet talk, eh?

Warsaw. Exactly, old menagerie.

Sharp. How would you like to invest about fifty dollars, say, in the circus—good security?

Warsaw. What am I going to do then?

Sharp. Just so; I'm anxious to make some repairs and change things a little. Now here's a fine openin' for you: you help me with fifty dollars and take an interest! See? Get the drift? Splendid, ain't it?

Warsaw. Well—yes—rather gorgeous—but too much like the rainbow.

Sharp. How's that?

Warsaw. You can't get it.

Sharp. Redicerlous! 'Spose we try it? 'spose you lend me fifty dollars jus' for an experiment?

Warsaw. My friend, I don't experiment with fifty dollar bills, I take ten-cent drinks.

Sharp. You're lettin' a splendid chance slip from you!

Warsaw. Theoretically your plan's feasible, but it's powerfully abstract.

Sharp. I say, lend me ten dollars—five dollars—one dollar then!

Warsaw (*rising*). You're honest, no doubt, but ask Sandy; here he is. Now for the music! (*exit*)

Enter Sandy.

Sharp. That feller talks slick, my stars!—Wanted to borrer fifty dollars from me!

Sandy. Is it posserble?

Sharp. Notwithstandin' he knew what my expenses must be! You know that!

Sandy. Of course I do! It's shameful. (*goes behind his counter*)

Sharp. Now for our bait. How is it?

Sandy. Gone, sir! gone!

Sharp. I would have swore to it! Ain't he a corruptin' feller?

Sandy. Now ain't he? The dog! what'll we do with him?

Sharp. It's mighty perplexin', but keep everything quiet for a time, and then we'll arrest him. We'll chuck him in jail to-morrer.

Sandy. You think that's best, eh?

Sharp. It's the only way, say nothin'. Are you certain you won't have any need for that ten dollar bill you lent me awhile ago?

Sandy. Oh! no, you'll pay it back to-morrer evenin'.

Sharp. Yes, I will. I'm goin' to take a trip in the country in the mornin', you know, to find out how the roads are. I'll be back in the evenin'.

Sandy. Yes, you told me that. Hush! Somebody's comin'. Jus' keep your seat and be mum. There!

Enter Warsaw, with his fiddle—Aleck Fury is stationed outside the door. Warsaw, having surveyed them both carefully, takes a seat just behind the tramp and begins to play the "Arkansas Traveller." Suddenly he stops and punches the tramp in the ribs with his fiddle-bow, and starts again quickly as if he hadn't done anything. Again he thrusts him in the ribs and resumes his playing without a variation of countenance. This is repeated till the tramp is exasperated.

Sharp (*rising, exasperated*). Well! I think you might let a gentleman alone, I do! (*sits down*)

Sandy. What is it? Anything wrong?

Sharp. Nothin', except he's pokin' me in the ribs! (*another thrust*) I say, can't you let me alone! That's six times! (*sits down again*)

Sandy (rising). I won't have this in my tavern! What is it?

Warsaw. Sit down, excited gawk! It's my old fiddle, that's all! (*begins to play again and then thrusts the tramp's hat down over his eyes*)

Sharp (to Sandy). Well, sir! you lose me as a boarder! By dad, it's too much! (*presently resumes his seat*)

Sandy. You sneakin' rogue! I'll tell you somethin'—

Warsaw. Sit down, I tell you! Let me soothe you!

Sandy. No, sir! I'm goin' to show you up!—The night you come here first, you emptied my till; you did the very same thing this mornin' and a little while ago! I'll give you partic'ler fits, you slippery rogue!

Warsaw (moving back within easy reach of the tramp's gripsack). Now, old man, give me your ears a minute. You remember, a bald-headed tramp robbed you on the first night and robbed me; that's proved; I wouldn't rob myself, of course! I've got the money you left in the till to-night—

Sandy. Aha! –

Warsaw. But the money you left there this morning, an insidious tramp has got.—Now here's the purse that Lucy lost; it came out of this carpet-bag; look, Sandy, look! (*turns the bag upside down so that the bricks fall out*) There's the rascal, grab him!

Sandy. My stars! I'm wrong! Oh! I've got you! (*rushes at Sharp who flings something like dust into his eyes*) Look out! pepper! pepper!

Warsaw (seizing a brick as the tramp rushes toward the door). Back, sir! back! you're euchred, sir! -Now Aleck!

Enter Aleck Fury, with his pistol.

Aleck. Aha! throw up your arms, sir! quick! I'll down you! (*the tramp does so*) Come on, Sandy, we'll tie his arms. (*they do so*)

Warsaw (thrusting him with his fiddle-bow). Well, sir! what have you got to say for yourself now?

Aleck. Yes, what do you mean by all this?

Sharp. I can't help it!

Warsaw. What! can't help stealing?

Sharp. No! I'm a kleptermaniac! (*at this point, Phil. Sly, who has been lurking about, thrusts his head in at the door.*)

Sly (*astonished*). Good-bye, Billy, I'm off for Texas! (*vanishes*)

Sandy. Ha! there's the other rogue! We'll swing to this one!

Warsaw. Yes, the deep-dyed villain with the baldhead! He's gone!—Be careful, Aleck, be careful; I once got away from a constable myself—

Aleck. You did? How was it?

Warsaw. I was arrested one day in July on a false charge. It was broiling hot, and the court-house was two miles off. Now the constable, instead of letting me go there in my buggy, tied my arms and started to walk me there. He was afraid I'd get away, you see—

Aleck. Yes—

Warsaw. Well, when we had gone about a mile and a quarter, the fellow got tired, and we stopped under a big oak tree to rest ourselves. The constable stretched himself on the grass and rolled over two or three times just for a change. Suddenly he rose to his feet with a shout, and gazed at me in breathless terror, his eyes rolling like a pair of infuriated moons. It was an appalling situation. Presently six yellow-jackets marched our from under his shirt—a moment more—he was off at a bound, flying down the road, his right arm working like the driving-wheel of a steam engine. He went humming through the air like a nail, and passed the first mile-post in less than three minutes; and then for an instant, I saw him in the remote distance like a speck, and he faded from sight and was seen no more! I tell you, boys, that fellow overtook a hurricane on the road!

Sharp. Ha! ha! ha! as I'm a sinner!

Warsaw. Away with that rusty tramp! Get your hat, Sandy! —Hello! Parson!

Enter Hezekiel Kent, very sleepy.

Kent. Well, who was it woke me up and told me to come

down to the Tavern this time o' night, anyhow?

Aleck. Why I did—for help.

Kent. You did? (*looking about*) Brother Sharp! how are you?

Sandy. Brother Sharp's goin' to leave us now? (*exeunt Sandy, Sharp, Aleck*)

Warsaw. He's a thief, Parson, that's all. You're mistaken,

Kent. Is it posserble? Well, well, ain't I mistaken now! Hey, here's them ladies, too, Trav'ler.

Enter Lucy and Agnes.

Warsaw. You're just too late.

Lucy. We are? So you've really caught him?

Agnes. That's splendid; we came down to see.

Warsaw. And we saw his friend, the old bald-headed tramp. He got away, Lucy, and left for Texas.

Lucy. The rascal!—Who is that yonder? (*pointing at Sam just entering*)

Warsaw. That looks like Sam.

Enter Sam Easy, just waked up from his nap.

Sam (*rubbing his eyes*). Hello! is that you, Parson? Are you goin' to fight too? Well, well, (*brightens up a little, then rolls up his sleeves carefully and squares himself off*) Now boys, I'm ready fetch in the tramp!

Warsaw. Just too late, Sam.

Sam. Too late? My sakes, have I overslep' myself? How'd I do that?

Kent. You're always behin' time; nobody counted on you.

Sam. Well, did *you* git here?

Warsaw. The Parson was late, too.

Sam (*drawing out a flask*). Have another drink, Parson?

Kent. I don't want it, sir!

Sam. Parson, it's a pity you drink! But let's shake hands anyhow (*they do*).

Warsaw (*at the door*). Here they come!

Lucy. Who?

Warsaw. Sandy and Aleck.

Enter Sandy and Aleck Fury.

Sandy. Here's your knife, Parson; we searched him. He confessed that another man named Sly robbed us on the first night and stole the purse in the Tavern.

Warsaw. Aha! so he put it in his carpetbag and forgot about it!

Kent. Well, well, here's my old knife. You've got him safe, eh?

Aleck. Yes, sir. we've got him safe in jail; that's the way to do- bizness—bizness—bizness! Let's have a song, boys!

Lucy. Oh! yes, come here now (*goes into Warsaw's pocket*). Here it is; you said you'd sing it; you must!

Warsaw. Oh! Lucy, I'm too modest, but I'll try. This is the song I sing to the gaping crowds, and I wrote it while driving down the banks of the Arkansas river. There was a man who, when he was made angry, reached for his pistol, and called it "My Percussion Cap," and so—

There lived a man in Junkertown,
The queerest I have seen;
His hair was white, his clothes were brown,
His specs were bottle-green.
He'd play casino, euchre, too,
And handled poker well,
And then he'd read the Bible through,
And take a pious spell!

CHORUS. But mind! it wouldn't do to scoff,
Or raise a laugh at him, my chap;
He'd frown, and then you'd best be off;
He'd reach for his percussion cap.

He dealt in 'possums Sunday morn,
In turtles, gophers, too;
And spent the midday hoeing corn,
And nodded in his pew.
He held the Gospel in one hand,
The world, sir, in the other!
He did it nicely—understand?
He worked them both together!

CHORUS. But mind! enough's enough, my friend,

He'd notify you, "Verbum sap!"
And if you didn't scamper then—
" By jove! where's my percussion cap!"

The boys would hold their tongues, from fear,
They knew him through and through;
And if he thought you meant to sneer,
He'd cast a leer at you.
He was a sinner, what's the use
To say he wasn't when he was?
I never told him he was loose,
I never did, because—

CHORUS. It wouldn't do, as I have said,
He'd warn you with a thunder-clap;
And then you'd hear him as you fled:
" Oh—yes, where's my percussion cap!"*

Such was the man in Junkertown,
The queerst I have seen;
Whose hair was white, whose clothes were brown,
Whose specs were bottle-green.

Sam. Toler'ble good! Your speakin' of gophers—

Agnes. Pray tell me, what is a gopher?

Sam. Georgia's the place for gophers, boys, 'way down in Georgia!

Warsaw. In the sorghum fields—

Sam. Wherever there is sorghum, there's gophers, or there ought to be, anyhow!

Lucy. Yes, but what is it, please?

Warsaw. Lend me your ears, Lucy, and I'll describe the party. Now observe, the turtle and the gopher appear to be close kin, at first sight, but they differ materially. Mark me, the turtle, you know, lives in the water and on the land—amphibious, you see—he's mixed in his notions; he eats dirt and drinks water. He can't help it—it's constitutional. A gopher, however, prefers

*You observe that the metre is stormy—at times; the last line of the chorus appears to have had a spasm. I got the knack from Charles Wesley.—AUTHOR.

terra firma; he abhors water from first principles—it's innate with him, ain't it, Sam?

Sam. I know it to be a fact, I'm somethin' of a boternist myself!

Agnes. Now I'm dreadfully mixed!

Sam. Yes, it takes study.

Sandy (*at the door*). Boys, boys, you don't know it, but the sun's up in the east!

Warsaw. It is? Then, Lucy, when all is ready, we will bid them good-bye, our friends of the Big Fork Tavern!

Lucy. Oh! Hiram, I will go with you in your buggy, Agnes and I!

Warsaw. And we shall see Kentucky together!

Sandy (*rushing up*). What, are you two goin' to be married? Why I didn't know all that was goin' on in my Tavern!

Aleck (*rushing up*). What's that?

Sandy. These two are goin' to git married.

Kent (*rushing up*) Is that so?

Agnes (*smiling*). Is it really true, sister?

Lucy. Why of course it is. I have chosen Hiram Warsaw.

Warsaw. Lucy, my girl, risk no other!

Sam (*struck by an idea*). Let's celerbrate it, boys! Where's that 'simmon beer?

[CURTAIN.]

www.ingramcontent.com/pod-product-compliance
Lightning Source LLC
Chambersburg PA
CBHW021444090426
42739CB00009B/1632
* 9 7 8 3 3 3 7 2 9 2 2 8 7 *